Deep Cuts

poems by

Steve Coughlin

Finishing Line Press
Georgetown, Kentucky

Deep Cuts

Publisher: Leah Huete de Maines
Editor: Christen Kincaid
Cover Art: Alex Linch, Credit: Getty Images/iStockphoto
Author Photo: Mike Coughlin
Cover Design: Elizabeth Maines McCleavy

Order online: www.finishinglinepress.com
        also available on amazon.com

Author inquiries and mail orders:
Finishing Line Press
P. O. Box 1626
Georgetown, Kentucky 40324
U. S. A.

Table of Contents

For John and Marie Coughlin

"Everybody's got a hungry heart."
—Bruce Springsteen

I

The Next Thirty-Two Years

Work starts at six a.m. You can arrive early but never arrive late. This is your workbench. It will always be your workbench. This is where you put your work gloves. You can place a photograph of your newborn son here or here, but not here—this spot is only for your work gloves. In twenty years your newborn son will be murdered. His skull will be cracked open by a tire iron. His body will be discovered between railroad tracks and a shoe factory. Here is the only machine you will ever work on. It makes quarter-inch gears. On the first of each month I will collect your union dues. Don't ever forget to pay your union dues. At the top of this stairwell is the roof. Instead of eating lunch, most days you will run five miles on top of the roof. Don't ever touch the quarter-inch gears—not even when wearing your work gloves. They burn hot for at least an hour. To pass the time you might want to watch the gears fade from red to silver. Here is a pair of goggles. They are not required. If you choose not to wear these goggles, they should always be hung from this hook. Don't bother to consider the uses of quarter-inch gears. Nobody bothers to consider the uses of the gears they make. Here is a stack of envelopes. They are for your union dues. When you go on vacation make sure to train your temporary replacement the wrong way to make quarter-inch gears. Have him pull this lever instead of this lever. This will make you almost irreplaceable. There is asbestos in the ceiling. There is asbestos in the walls. Your doctor will inform you that asbestos could be the reason you get throat cancer the year after you are laid off. There will be surgery that removes half your larynx, you will speak in a whisper for the rest of your life. But that's in thirty-three years. These are the men who work on the floor below yours. They will never learn your name—you will never learn theirs. When we go on strike in fifteen years you will picket next to these men. Even though they will not speak to you, by then you'll understand we are in this together. Days will drag by slow, each gear no different from the last. You will learn to hate quarter-inch gears. But don't complain. There are men who have worked here much longer who have earned the right to complain. When your son dies the union will send you a bouquet of flowers. This is one of the benefits of belonging to a union. The company will not send you flowers. The company will require you to fill out a bereavement form. The union is the reason you'll get a week to grieve. Remember, if it wasn't for the union you would not get this. Our bouquet will be placed right beside your son's casket.

Endless Night

How could we not have wanted you
to remain at the factory—
                                your late shift never
to end, the building empty
except for you? How could it not have been better
if you wandered forever
past the factory's silent machines, the threat
of their metal teeth resting, the stillness
of work gloves on workbenches? And always,
during each endless
minute, the sound of your boot steps
would echo on the concrete floor
sounding so different
from your sleepless nights walking through our house
heavy with alcohol. You'd have wandered
past rows of safety
goggles hung from hooks, past the break room's
fluorescent light—the janitor never arriving
at five a.m. to empty
the trash, never dumping out the tin ashtrays forever
filled with ash.

                        Instead of you shaking me
awake in the blue-black night, your sleeplessness
becoming my sleeplessness, demanding I listen
to your complaints about your wife—
desperate for her own sleep—
no longer allowing you into her bed,
how could we not have wanted
your car to remain alone
in the parking lot, the factory's red-brown brick
barely visible in the moonless sky?
Hours later morning would arrive
for us—not you—and we'd sit at the kitchen table
well rested, my schoolbag on the floor,
never recognizing your empty seat.

It would just be you shaking
locked exit doors, wandering past dirty restrooms
and vending machines, past beat-up
lockers filled with sweat-stained clothes, wandering
into offices filled with stacks of unsigned papers,
calendars with meetings circled in red,
black telephones without dial tones

but still you'd place the mouthpiece
against your lips, still your voice
would call out your wife's name
or maybe mine—how could I not have wanted this?

Haunted

He was the bedroom, the Black Sabbath poster thumbtacked to the wall. He was the unmade twin bed and dirty sheets my grieving mother refused to wash. He hovered outside the second-story window. My dead brother watching as I turned out his lamp. He'd press his twenty-one-year-old hands against the glass, fingers pale and stiff, as I stacked his two thin pillows. He was the black and red blanket covering my shoulders, my sudden sweat-drenched waking. I heard his shallow breathing, searched for his shadow beyond the moon's thin line. His mind schizophrenic. His hand, I imagined, grasping a box cutter. I waited for him to walk toward me. He was the loneliness in the months after his death, my father leaving each day for work. There was the silence that followed visitors when they entered the house. There were the excuses they offered each time to leave. He was the bathroom door dangling from a hinge, the fan in the den with a broken blade. He was my sister hiding in her bedroom. I sat in his seat at the kitchen table. My mother, desperate for her dead son to return, placing before me his cracked white plate and orange drinking glass. Each morning he walked beside me on the sidewalk, his breath drifting into the cold air. He followed me down the hallways at school—in fourth grade, fifth grade—my older brother, his long hair unwashed, waiting outside my classroom door. There was the mustache he grew the months before his death. There was the frayed denim jacket hanging from his shoulders, a pack of cigarettes sticking out the front pocket. My brother the murdered drug dealer. My brother, his mind a terrifying mess, laughing as I walked the train tracks, balancing on the rails, tossing rocks at windows. He watched me shatter bottles on the street. He told me to run and keep running when a neighbor's voice called for me to stop. I was him sitting on the couch refusing to talk. I was him flipping stations desperate to escape, my foot tapping, my fingers drumming on the remote. And when I tried to sleep, when I closed my eyes, I could feel him inside my mind. He said my thoughts were his thoughts. He said I too would fall apart—that my confused mind would also make me light a fire in the school's dumpster. He was the hockey stick leaning against the bedroom wall. He was the hockey skates abandoned in the closet. I could feel him in the darkness, his hand about to touch my shoulder. I sensed the coldness of his skin. I heard the softness of his voice. He was the sleep that wouldn't come.

The Idea of North

David's dead father's car points like a compass needle—driving North past years of construction on Boston's Tobin Bridge, miles of auto lots, my own father's favorite restaurant on the Route 1 strip. This is three weeks after David's eulogy about his dead father tossing a baseball with him in their backyard. This is January. David driving his dead father's car past lobster shacks closed for the season, billboards for steakhouses and Chinese restaurants. Past Salisbury and Seabrook. We do not stop at the discount liquor store as David's father would have. We do not stop at the greasy diner, order a hamburger and fries, like my father. Past the Maine state line. David weaves his dead father's car past snow banks three feet high, pulls onto I-95 to merge with eighteen-wheelers hauling lumber. After stopping at a gas station, opening a bag of potato chips, we do not discuss returning home. We drive past Orono listening to a dead man's CDs. Past Dyer Brook in a car that is not my father's. My father who abuses my mother. My father who leans his burning face into hers, blames her for every failed decision he's made. I do not tell David that he is at home watching television. My father who runs five miles a day—fifty pushups, a hundred sit-ups. Hours of moose crossing signs. Hours of silence as we drive without a destination, the Canadian border seventy miles away. If there's an idea of North it's in the sleet now falling—the highway threatening us with the inevitability of ice. It's buried under miles of evergreen trees, arctic tundra, snow that never melts. David's dead father's car pushes into a wind that feels North. The heater cranking. This dead man's car with a dead man's winter coat in the backseat. A dead man's cancer that never wrecked my father's body. A dead man's drinking that also led to abuse—our thoughts circle this but we do not know how to discuss it. North which is night and a dirty windshield, stars hidden during a winter storm. North which is not my father waking me on a July morning when I am seven, carrying me to the car for a family vacation. My father who this time does not intimidate with anger but covers me with a blanket. His baseball glove packed next to mine. David's father who will no longer walk into their backyard, pick a baseball up off the ground. I listen to the heater in this car that is not my father's. I lean toward the warmth as David stares into darkness.

In Defense of the McDonald's Corporation as Represented by Ronald McDonald

You were there, Ronald, Thursday nights, the good times
of your golden arches glowing
through winter's interminable night, my mother, twenty pounds
overweight, indulging in ten Chicken McNuggets. I could have sat forever
in one of your booths by the windows
while my father worked a double shift, our kitchen's scuffed floor
so different from the wet gleam
of your recently mopped tiles. I clung to the safety of the families
surrounding us where my father could never
drink himself into a rambling rant
about my mother refusing to cook the family dinner.
In truth, it was impossible to take an interest
in the absurdity of your yellow jump suit, your red-white sleeves
like a swirling barber's pole. I simply craved
the deep-fried goodness of your french fries. I yearned each Thursday
to escape to the oozing warmth
of your baked apple pie
where I whisked away dinner debris
on a small brown tray. Let my mother, her rigid perm
adding ten years, forever sip
one of your supersized soft drinks. Let cholesterol
clog her arteries, the extra calories a small concession
to escape my father's empty beer cans
in the living room. Your soothing milkshake
allowed her to avoid the constant cloud of blame—
the hallway carpet she never vacuumed, the kitchen oven
she seldom turned on—that followed her
even while he was at work. Let my mother who lived
in that house like a prisoner
watch me delight in another plastic Happy Meal toy.
Let her reach across the table to again
take my hand, the final threads of youth
in her smile, so many hours
from my father's car pulling into the driveway,
from him opening the porch screen door,
as the sound of families surround us
promising everything will be okay.

Window Cracked Open

Thousands of days turning the engine, striking a match, backing
her rusted Ford Escort out of the driveway. Thousands of errands

to the grocery store, the post office, with the window cracked open,
heater rattling, winter's chill rushing in. My mother cradles a cigarette

between her fingers, taps ash into the street. She tastes
menthol on her lips and tongue—inhales a smoke-filled breath

deep into her lungs. A few minutes to escape
the half-frozen chicken thawing on the counter, the rotary telephone

that never rings. Through the two-inch slit she hears brakes squeal
from melted snow, watches exhaust drift into the dull sky.

And maybe, Mom, I'm just home from school, eleven years old, removing my
boots on the porch as you drive past the discount liquor store, the half-filled

Kmart parking lot, or maybe I'm in high school walking from the bus stop
too concerned with the girl beside me to notice your taillights.

A few minutes away from kids slamming the kitchen door, tossing backpacks
on the floor; from *The Brady Bunch* on the living room television,

music blasting and feet thumping upstairs. She craves the subtle burn
at the back of her throat, ignores her right hand red and numb

as she grips the wheel. A few minutes to imagine the warmth
of a different car—brand new, roof down—she could drive far from here.

She passes empty storefronts on Main Street, the abandoned shoe factory
on Jefferson. She lights a second cigarette after turning onto Market

though our house is only a mile away. A few minutes to desire
release from this wind, from these gusts of snow. A few minutes

to be with this man she imagines beside her—this man so perfectly
not my father, who is no particular man at all

but the kindness of a hand on her leg as she cruises
what must be the California seaside, the lights of a boardwalk Ferris wheel

in the distance, or somewhere in the desert under an oasis of sky,
the Sangre de Cristo Mountains before her, as the radio finally plays a summer tune

and your cigarette, Mom, the one between your fingers,
is only a small part of so much more.

My Father's Recitation

My father ran through my mother's heart attack. He ran through the afternoon my sister was hit by a car—her femur bone cracked in four places. During the Blizzard of '78 my father stood on the porch and ran in place for eighty-five minutes. During the Blizzard of '91, instead of leaving work while the roads were passable, my father ran up and down eight flights of stairs. He spent the night at the factory on a concrete floor. The morning my older brother's unconscious body was found, skull bashed in, drug deal gone wrong, my father ran to his beat-up Mercury from his quarter-inch gear machine where he made miniature gears for boat engines. His brain ran so loud he could almost drown out the doctor's voice. "One, two, three," my father kept repeating. His watch counted each second. His notebooks, his volumes of notebooks, recorded the distance of each run, the weather and location. My mother, her skin a colorless white, knocked on the bedroom wall, kept calling his name, but my father, clinging to his numbers, was running loops around the high school track. He bought a new wristwatch, another pair of sneakers. He ran with swollen knees, walked like a zombie unable to bend his legs. He ran through alcohol addiction, through depression so heavy a short run was the only reason to get out of bed. Past Stop signs, past Yield signs, past Do Not Enter signs. Drivers flipped him off after slamming their brakes. "One, two, three," my father explained. Was it the day of an election, the Challenger explosion? The Thursday my brother was expelled from school for lighting a fire behind the gym? My father's notebook observes, "6.9 miles / Mostly cloudy / Iced knees thirty minutes." Monday I delivered newspapers. Tuesday I delivered newspapers. I pedaled my bike and tried to join his recitation: "One, two, three." In twelfth grade I averaged six-minute miles. I kneeled on one leg and vomited on the sidewalk. I curled into a ball and waited for the shaking to stop. Never a discussion of shallow breathing, my mother's chest tight as a fist. Never a follow-up appointment with the doctor. Just my father running through the cemetery, past the polished granite of his son's stone. His numbers keeping pace with each long stride.

II

It

How can I describe the arrival of It
in Bill's Jeep Grand Cherokee during a June night in 1995?
We drove away from my white house filled
with my aging parents
but for us there was the swirling promise
of Nantasket's shoreline—It assuring us
that all the girls
their laughter floating like waves
would finally notice as we drove by.

It was the same It
which appeared to me and Tamara years later
at Massiminos in Boston. It suggested
we order chocolate trifle for dessert.
It—in the form of two more glasses of zinfandel—
insisted every square inch
of the city, each brick on the Freedom Trail,
was only meant for us.

I imagine It at the Louvre revealing Itself
like the Madonna to a tourist
who witnesses in *The Wedding Feast at Cana* something more
than just a masterpiece. Bill turned up Toad the Wet Sprocket's
"All I Want" because It stated this was the only song
the universe wanted to hear. I waved to the girl
in grey Chuck Taylors
because It assured me she would wave back.

And always the addictive chase of It.
My father ran day after day hoping to reclaim
It's elusive high. Bill again played "All I Want"
and we dutifully sang "The air outside so soft
is saying everything"

but we were driving home
and It was further away
than any of the girls we had stared at.

And where is It now?
My father, too old to run, walks two hours a day.
I stay up each night
searching for new shows on Netflix.

And still my father wanders the rooms of his house.
It gone from those nights
he stays up after midnight. Gone too from the bedroom
that once contained his wife.
My father counted the minutes left in his shift
just to return to their bed. How he whispered
her name to see if she had waited.
How her body turned toward his.
It no longer promising that this is all he'll ever need.

The Sound of Twilight

In the glow of almost-night it sounds
nothing like the thud of the kitchen oven,
my mother's footsteps
on cold linoleum. Standing on the front porch steps,
head tilted forward, my father doesn't recognize
my ten-year-old voice calling
our dog's name in the backyard
but hears the soothing undulations
of the beach's surf
ten miles away. Beyond the living room television that blares
for no one, he listens
to the carousel's ceaseless yearning
twenty years ago, his '62 convertible
cruising the strip.

                    In this light
that's beyond light, my father—hand suspended
above the door handle—does not hear
the broken faucet's guttural cough
but embraces the aching guitar in "Blue Velvet"
drifting from a seaside barroom, the neon exclamation
of Old Milwaukee
and the voice of a love
that never complains of unpaid bills.

Again the sound of quarters dropping
into the juke. Again the soft brush of lips
against his ear.

                    After decades of waking at four a.m.
my father doesn't hear me call to him
from the porch asking if everything is okay
as these final wisps of light
promise he'll never grow old
and Bobby Vinton once more sings "Warmer than May
her tender sighs."

　　　　　　Or maybe it's only her voice
he leans toward, the soft rustle
of her dress. Maybe it's only the lightness of her whisper—
his name alive on her lips—that keeps him
on the steps like stone
as I keep calling
and he fades into a darkness that feels so right.

Deep Cuts

"From his bad complexion to hopeless fashion sense, no pop singer of the 90s was more uncool-cool than Michael Stipe."
　　　—Paste Magazine

I accept, Sienna Jenkins, you did not watch the MTV world premiere music video of R.E.M.'s "What's the Frequency, Kenneth" in September 1994. I also accept

that upon watching the video and noticing R.E.M.'s lead singer, Michael Stipe, had shaved his head you would not have stood in front of the bathroom vanity

ashamed by the awkwardness of your teenage self before recklessly buzzing away all traces of hair. Maybe, Sienna, you didn't search every thrift store

in a thirty-mile radius desperate to locate the same olive-green with large red star t-shirt Michael Stipe wore in the video or devote your evenings after dinner

to singing along with Michael to several of R.E.M.'s deepest cuts. But what I'm struggling to accept, Sienna, is how when I stood before you

in my not-quite-olive-green t-shirt featuring several mustard colored stars and my bald head shinning fiercely it was not just my suggestion

we attend the Forever 80s semi-formal together you rejected but just as importantly it felt as if you had rejected the entirety

of my Michael-Stipe-I-too-can-be-cool-even-if-I-don't-look-cool fixation. And I guess, Sienna, I can't really accept any of this.

Maybe you want to insist you only sat in front of me during second period biology and seldom offered more than a thoughtful hello. Maybe you think it's unreasonable

for me to believe you were secretly attracted to the sweat-stained orange and black R.E.M. visor I wore attempting to evoke Michael Stipe's uncool-coolness.

Honestly, Sienna, how could you not get a vibe of my Michael Stipe potential? Did you miss it when I hummed "The One I Love" each morning behind you?

Can't you admit you were not simply being kind when you returned my smile
in the hallway? Can't you confess you recognized an alluring profundity

beyond my pasty skin and pockmarked face? Can't you finally confide
you were at least slightly tempted by my scrawny frame

so similar to Michael Stipe's scrawny frame? The same Michael Stipe
who confidently gripped the microphone in my mind to reveal an inner depth

as 20,000 fans cheered his utter uncoolness and who convinced me, Sienna,
you desired all that I am.

What Gets Lost

"The last good kiss you had was years ago."
—Richard Hugo

It's more about the years.
You could fill a block of abandoned houses
with books read, but no other woman
has cost you sleep for the taste
of her skin. And please admit,
work has not been good—
seven years packing cameras
in a warehouse. *Was it even real,*
that kiss? You couldn't find it
in the novels of Theodore Dreiser,
or sleeping under a tree
in southern Georgia.

Years have taken her voice,
her skirt is left—ocean blue.
The summer night
no longer has its day, the music
has lost its guitar.

Even the months—
how many had heartbeats
that made you feel the color red?
Before dinner you walk the house
searching boxes for letters
signed with her name.
Nights have taken earrings, bracelets.
And at midnight, last night,
you couldn't even remember her.
Just lips, their color almost gone.

To the 1990s

What a decade you were!
When you began I was a preteen seldom missing a Wednesday night viewing

of *Doogie Howser, M.D.* but by your end I dedicated most Wednesday nights
to trading Blind Melon songs with Bill Traverse

at the Rivershed Tavern. In your early part
I watched *Edward Scissorhands*—my first Winona Ryder film—

and by 1996 I had an entire bedroom wall devoted to Winona.
With a decade-sized spotlight you revealed the necessity of black combat boots

and faded ripped jeans. It was during you I stole
countless thrift store t-shirts from my older brother's closet

several sizes too large. It was also during you
I bought Alanis Morissette's piercingly-jaded *Jagged Little Pill.*

Do you remember that afternoon in 1998 when I showed up two hours late
to my sister's surprise party because I could not stop blasting

Alanis' "You Oughta Know?" And always there was Winona:
Winona portraying an erotically charged Mina Harker

in *Bram Stoker's Dracula*; Winona offering an understated performance
as a synthetic droid in *Alien Resurrection.*

And since I was only a few years removed from you in 2003
for my twenty-fifth birthday I requested my parents purchase me

a boxset of the early 90s dramedy *Northern Exposure.*
And after moving to Idaho in 2005 when winter

was a fifty-pound weight I wore the same plaid shirt
I bought at The Garment District in 1997. I'm not sure, 1990s,

if you're aware of the 2016 Netflix original series *Stranger Things*
but Winona once more has a leading role. She plays a single mother

instead of a rebel-goth-teen in *Welcome Home, Roxy Carmichael*
but like the subway car I rode in 1998 she leads me through decades

of unwanted passing. And when I returned to Alanis' *Jagged Little Pill* in 2017
there was a moment when I was again in my childhood bedroom

jamming out to "You Oughta Know." And now it's 2018
and students enter my classroom without the slightest interest

for Winona's Oscar nominated performance in *Little Women.*
They insist instead upon the shimmering glow of their own decade

not understanding how incomparable it is to the pale perfection
of Winona's skin in *The Age of Innocence*; nothing like the steadfast loyalty

Winona's May offered Daniel Day-Lewis' Archer
during the complicated months of their courtship.

Nothing like Winona—*our Winona*—who smiled with such devotion
it was clear you'd never have to end.

His Youth

Decades before he folded her sweaters into a trash bag, placed them on a curb in front of the house, his youth rumbled with desire as she washed dishes in a yellow dress, sunlight crawling across the kitchen floor.

It was trips to the beach in his Ford convertible, the scent of salt water—the parking lot melting beneath their feet.

At twenty-seven he woke beside her in the coldness of morning, their clothes discarded on the floor, stifled a yawn as he dressed for the factory. There were the cement stairs he bounded two at a time, the shifts when he worked a machine that produced an endless stream of miniature gears.

It was him in the break room repeating the same jokes to men whose names he never learned.

And maybe a few minutes before the whistle blew he walked to the payphone in his grease-stained shirt.

Maybe he deposited his only quarter just to hear her voice.

Years before his DUI, it was him stumbling drunk into bed, the darkness spinning him wildly to sleep.

At thirty-one he could not explain to her how his youth, its relentless demands, was the restlessness that kept him driving alone into the night.

Was there an affair in a cheap motel room? Was there whiskey and cigarettes on the nightstand—his need to touch another woman's body?

Did his wife, hours later, her own youth lost to depression, her body grown fat, allow him to wrap his arm around her? Did she ignore the perfume on his skin as he pulled her against his chest?

Before he was left to wander the empty rooms of his house, there was the embarrassment she felt when he revved the car's engine in the church's parking lot.

There was the eternity of minutes she waited in the car while he, forty-five, flirted with high school girls working at Dairy Queen.

And what if his youth became the shadow in front of him at fifty-four? What if it ran around the corner as his lungs burned?

There was the hopelessness of aching knees at sixty-six, the years he had gone since sleeping beside her in the same bed.

But after she told him of the cancer there were those final flares. It was youthful naiveté that convinced him she could get better. It was him insisting she eat a salad each night with dinner. Him helping her into the car for a drive to the ocean.

Before her heart stopped beating. Before her body cooled in front of him. Before he walked the lonely streets, legs too worn for running, eyes squinting, searching in the distance for the shadow.

How he grasped her tired hand.

Final Encore

I did not know, Youth, what to do when I had you.
It was as if every moment was Friday night
and there was no point if I was not driving my newest used car
incredibly fast. Now it's like we are in an emptying ballroom
under antique chandeliers
and you are in a wrinkled prom dress
a wilted corsage on your wrist
as I watch the band members return guitars to their cases
hoping for one final encore. It feels good
when you lead me into the hallway
because this must be one of many well-lit hallways
in this mansion on a bluff
high above the ocean. Though the walls
no longer feature posters of R.E.M. and Winona Ryder
at least on the polished tile floor
a black boombox plays Weezer's "My Name is Jonas."
When we descend the staircase and you point
toward the heated indoor swimming pool
just beyond the grand marble foyer
I feel less bothered by the firm bodies
of these twenty-year-olds
than the attention they take for granted—the dignified butler
hands clasped behind his back
maintaining order with occasional nods
footmen scurrying like ants
to refill empty Solo cups with cheap beer.
Hand on my shoulder
you guide me past the billiard room
where teenage boys play eight ball
and the study where graduate students
sit around a long oak table deciphering Derrida
as the antique grandfather clock, its long silver pendulum swinging,
announces the hour.
And it is late.
So late the party is over
as you gently lead me from your mansion
to this veranda

which features several Adirondack chairs
and a pleasant view of the ocean
and where a distant foghorn calls
as lights on the horizon wave gently
and where you for the last time
rest your head upon my shoulder.

III

The History of Longing

Evolution

The world began in darkness with a cluster
of microbes arguing, telling each other
where to shove things, until almost by accident

there was a touch. Out of hunger came the arm,
hand, lips—the tongue.

In the late Cambrian era a not-quite-human thing
crawled from the water and looked upon a woman.
She slept in a mango tree, and even though its lips

couldn't form the word desire, nothing could stop
this creature from wanting to climb the branches
and sleep beside her.

The Middle Ages

War covered the globe like a king-size blanket.
Everyone was overwhelmed with despair except

for a lady in black who listened to classical jazz.
Every night Lord Trollope wrote letters

to which she'd never respond. During the battle
of Ludford Bridge a sword ripped a hole

the size of London in his chest. Most soldiers agreed
that the cry Lord Trollope gave while falling to the ground

was not one of pain but of relief.

Astronomy

Every Tuesday Galileo would drink
at Downtown Joe's and talk
about the planet he loved. He said she owned

a blue dress which twice a week
she'd have laundered at Kip's Dry Cleaners.

He said she bathed by the light of her two moons—
that she'd slip out of her bathrobe and climb
into water so hot it would burn

anyone but her. After finishing his last drink
Galileo would stare into his empty glass,
frozen in thought, wondering why

she'd always let him watch but never
come close enough to touch.

Georgia

General Sherman torched Atlanta because
a man shouldn't have to be 6'1 just to get a date.

He watched mothers flee the city carrying
their children like grocery bags. He listened
to the pleas of the mayor and then hanged him

from a telegraph pole. The only building Sherman
left standing was a house in the Prescott district.
It rested on a hill with a woman inside

reading a book by Milton. At no point
did she seem concerned with the cries from below
which rose past her chimney

to climb like curses toward heaven.

Realism

For over twenty years Thomas Eakins painted
the same face. In the summer he'd stand

before the canvas and understand everything
about her lips; on Thursday mornings he could always

catch the right shade of her eyes. But Eakins
could never paint her hair which flowed

like an ocean he'd never seen; and somehow
her skin had a tone which ran outside

the realm of color. During his days
of retirement Eakins denied everything

about it. The paintings had long been destroyed
and he only wanted the world to forget

that once there was a face he knew so well
but could never fully capture.

Myth

Every day he followed as she'd pick oranges
in the orange grove and eat cherries underneath
the unnamed stars. Adam tried to tell her

she was doing it wrong, but still she ate bananas
for breakfast and kiwi for lunch.
One Sunday in late May he met with the serpent

and together they agreed something should be done.
But the next morning Adam woke after the sun
only to see her slipping out the garden gate.

Even with an unknown world before her
she didn't slow when he called out her name,
when Adam pleaded for her to return
as he stood alone under the apple tree.

IV

Preferable

I admit it was me who reached to the far back of the Safeway cooler to select
        the half-gallon carton of low-fat milk because it featured three extra
        days before expiration.
And yes, I was the shopper who invested several minutes trying to decide
        between half-frozen avocados.

Did you say my new tennis shoes glow with a blandness that lacks imagination?
Did you say I am even more predictable after signing up for online banking?

But what if I didn't turn the car around at twenty, middle of the night, when I
        briefly considered escaping my Boston life for the possibilities of
        Hollywood?
Look at that me surfing Malibu waves—a shamrock tattoo on each of my
        chiseled shoulders, my muscled stomach firm as an iron shield—as my
        part-time personal assistant, Hernando Champagne, watches me
        perform a perfectly executed double aerial barrel roll.
Did you say you've never heard of a double aerial barrel roll?
Did you even know I am considering an intriguing cameo in the new
        Terrence Malick film?
And did you hear I assisted Terrence with several key changes in the script
        as we ate dinner at Chi Spacca?
Yes, that was us sharing an appetizer of marinated baby artichokes when Martin
        Scorsese entered and once again informed us of his latest adventures
        with Leonardo DiCaprio. "Oh, Marty," I laughed, "None of us even care
        about your latest adventures with Leo."
And if you were privileged enough to see through the tinted windows of that
        luxury limousine, you would discover I am just one of five trusted
        members of the Winona Ryder Golden Ticket Entourage.
But even that me wants to be home by nine.
When Winona taps my knee, her hair again styled into a tousled shag
        as it was in the 1994 film *Reality Bites*, and asks if I want to accompany
        them back to her Sunset Boulevard mansion for an early evening
        swim in her recently renovated salt water swimming pool,
        I look down at my watch and say, "Maybe next time."

Preferable my closet of monochrome button-up shirts.
Preferable too my three indistinguishable pairs of beige khakis.

But what about this other me who moved to San Francisco at twenty-five?
Did you know I was hired by Italian fashion guru Robert Cavalli to wander the
        city modeling his latest designs?
Do you see me in a cream-white single-breasted blazer with dual back vents
        sauntering along Sea Cliff Avenue?
Look at how I enter a new favorite bar in North Beach.
Look at that table of young female professionals overwhelmed by the aura
        of my presence.
But after a few days, just when the bartender with neon-purple hair begins pouring
        my Midshipman Top of the Hops IPA with accompanying shot of
        Uncle Jack's Turkey Vulture Bourbon before I even order, I choose to
        stay home worn down by the city's unyielding rush.

Preferable watching a baseball game on the television.
Preferable these blue basketball shorts, white t-shirt.
Look at how I resist going to the Old Main for a single beer.
Watch how I stay in my living room as another car, windows down, speeds
        westward.

Strides

How pleasant you are today northwest Nebraska!—
like tough-guy
John Wayne singing "Red Wing" in *The Shootist*.

Here I am bundled
in my Calvin Klein winter coat
prepared for your late-March bluster
and there you are more appealing than Jane Russell's bodice
in *The Outlaw*.
I adore your miles of empty grassland
and badlands rugged as a John Ford film—I could walk for weeks
in your dry creeks
without encountering a single Walmart greeter!

Did you know of the years I lived in an eastern city?
The nights I circled
the same block of tenements
unable to find a parking space?
How better to indulge in your nothingness
the idea of riding horseback
with John Wayne tall in the saddle
masculinity flowing like whiskey.

To hell with watching *Once Upon a Time in the West*!
Just me and John Wayne and you
northwest Nebraska
my home on the edge of the West—our silence
impressive as any of your wind-worn buttes.

But for lunch
instead of John Wayne
offering me another hardtack biscuit
wouldn't it be better if hidden
in one of your wavy hills
was a Cracker Barrel restaurant?
Wouldn't it be preferable
for me and the Duke to tie our horses to a hitching post

and recline in rocking chairs
to eat the Big Boy Country Breakfast?

And after my third cup of coffee
it's back to your endless prairie
repetitive, really, as searching for a parking space
so after another hour why not surprise me
with a tumbleweed-blowing-swinging-door-saloon
Wild West town
featuring a newly constructed Barnes and Noble?
Instead of actually experiencing your Sandhills
Willa Cather will sing their brilliance!
And when John Wayne says, "Pilgrim,
we're burning daylight"
then, northwest Nebraska, I will jingle jangle
back into you. I will look upon the distant shadows of Crow Butte
and feel compelled
to bound across you with giant strides!

And after John Wayne and I get settled in our room
at the Best Western
oh, God, northwest Nebraska, how wonderful
it will be for the both of us
to unwind in our separate beds
a newly purchased ten-gallon hat on my head
and watch a double feature
of *My Darling Clementine* and *The Ox-Bow Incident*
or *The Wild Bunch* and *The Gunfighter*
or *High Noon* and *A Fist Full of Dollars*
as we drink too much whiskey
and smoke too many cigarillos
and marvel as if by firelight
about everything we love about the West.

Golden Age

It's how we sat by the picture window of Pat and Marv's Coffee House
drinking large vanilla lattes with caramel drizzle and how 1970s
country music danced and swayed among metal tables
and plastic flowers in overly-sized flowerpots and past the tacky mural
of enormous coffee beans in enormous wooden crates
and how the solitary barista in her stained apron serving a stream
of college students had set the volume just right.

And so much of it was each thread of Tamara's green jean jacket
that she bought at the mall out on Franklin with far too few parking
spaces but where Tamara wandered from Nordstrom to Macy's
in search of such a jean jacket and how Tamara's brown-blonde hair
touched her shoulders and the years of practice—the hundreds of
female heads with long female hair—Tamara's stylist must have
struggled with before achieving such success.

Yet it also was us agreeing despite this being only our third date
and the couple beside us having a loud disagreement
Santa Fe with its delectable New Mexican cuisine and invigorating
Margarita Trail must soon be visited as somewhere around our metal
chairs floated the possibility of Santa Fe's Georgia O'Keeffe Museum
and us considering with heightened admiration each of O'Keeffe's
lonesome skull paintings.

And when we walked by Sigmund's Creek with its soda cans and fast food
wrappers shining in sunlight it felt as if we were strolling along the
Italian Riviera with a yellow parasol in Tamara's hand.

And when we bought tickets at the Loring Hall—ceiling cracked, walls peeling—
it felt as if the building deserved recognition as an Undeniably
Significant Place.

And as we reclined in our torn plush seats it did not matter what formulaic film
we were about to watch because this clearly was the golden age
of mediocre cinema and the golden age of overly-salted popcorn
and even as darkness dropped around us we anticipated—we couldn't
stop—being bathed in so much light.

Song of the Almost-Sacred

I believe in Father Barry instructing us to repeat the Our Father until the
congregation's recitation was composed of authentic devotion, him
kneeling before the Holy Tabernacle for ten minutes, mid-August, the
hundred-year-old church a sweatbox of Sunday clothes.

I believe in Sarah Ellis waving as I rode my bicycle past her on the sidewalk
in tenth grade, two days before the Fourth of July, Sarah dressed in an
arousingly short red, white, and blue skirt.
I believe I was so gratified by her attention I had to return home and run wind
sprints in the backyard until supper.

And now it is Sunday morning and I don't believe Tamara's aware how enthralled
I am with her sleeping shorts. How I delight in her bare legs, the scent of
her damp hair, as she cuts a pepper for an omelet.

After Tom Carter graduated from divinity school we acknowledged the
permanent solemnity of his celebratory angel wings tattoo, the divine
detail of each feather stretching like the Rosary across his back, but
it never approached the almost-sacredness of a four-hour date with Nora
to Mama Maria's—Nora ordering us a third round of cosmopolitans, our
heads light as cherubs in the sky.
Let there be harvest salad and veal porterhouse and peach tart for dessert!
Let Nora's nails be painted yellow, her thin lips a blushing pink!
Let Mama Maria frown as I drag a heavy wooden chair around the table to lean
closer to each of Nora's words.

And still Father Barry drones on, still he holds the Eucharist before us.
I believe each infinite minute I kneeled in the pew my sixteen-year-old knees
yearned for the perpetually-promised sacred.

Yet somehow it was enough to follow Sarah Ellis after biology class and feel fulfilled
by her wrinkled sweatshirt.
So what if it never culminated in us holding hands along the Nantasket boardwalk.
Let Nora, her black dress clinging to her hips, not invite me into her fifth-floor
apartment.
Let me acknowledge that I was relieved not having to confront the expectations
of transcendence through sexual fulfillment.

I believe Father Barry, dead twenty years, has yet to finish mass.
I believe I will forever wait in line for Communion, the chalice hovering eternally
    before me.

I believe it must be better to sit with Tamara at the kitchen table.
Tamara in the warm morning light offering me a taste of her spicy Mexican omelet.
Tamara humming along with Lucinda Williams.
Tamara who so sweetly receives my romantic advances—yet for now let me only
    lean toward her, our bodies not quite touching, as church bells call
    in the distance.

Seven Ways of Looking at Saint Teresa

I.

Among Alba de Dios' twenty empty rooms
the only moving thing is a saw
cutting through the left wrist of Saint Teresa.

II.

The scent of lilies fills General Francisco Franco's bed chamber
as he no longer clings to life
but only the collarbone of Saint Teresa.

III.

What should one make of this November wind?
Is it a mother calling out for her missing child?
Or is it Saint Teresa calling out for her stolen heart?

IV.

A man and a woman
are one.
A man and a woman and the right leg of Saint Teresa
are five to fifteen years in the state penitentiary.

V.

I do not know which to prefer,
Van Gogh's *Green Ears of Wheat* with its thick, promising roses;
or the lungs of Saint Teresa hammered to the wall beside it
with heavy, copper nails.

VI.

The streets are crowded.
Pieces of Saint Teresa's alabaster foot must be selling for half-off.

VII.

In this small wooden box I keep the heart of Saint Teresa.
Although fainter now, when held tight enough it's still possible
to feel it beating, pumping faith through the veins of a disbeliever.
Here—I'm giving it to you.

The New Physics

My father was dead when he came to Napa for a visit.

We carried in his luggage and he sat down to have a slice of Tamara's chilled strawberry pie.

We drank coffee, he talked about work, and the next day we went for a drive along the Mendocino coast.

This isn't the first of my father's *appearances* and Larry's been offering his opinion that it has something to do with space-time relativity.

He says my father has an irrational way of understanding the universe and has been living for years in four-dimensional reality.

But theories like this only go so far in explaining how my father has been waking without the slightest hint of a heartbeat.

For over fifteen years he's been disappearing for months returning with nothing but missing teeth.

Local papers have speculated that perhaps my father's ability to defy death is proof of Penrose's black hole theory.

Jim says in 1957 the many-worlds interpretation predicted the possibility of someone like my father accomplishing this sort of feat.

Even Bell's theorem, Jim says, which only recently has been received by science, suggests life and death are a matter of perspective.

But when my father came to Napa it was the middle of summer.

We grilled hamburgers in the backyard and opened a bottle of chardonnay.

That night Cameron and Stacey stopped by sometime after two and once again it all came back to subatomic particles and Max Planck and for a few moments they shared a heated debate over the supposed shortcomings of the S-matrix.

Come morning Cameron still couldn't let go of the quantum mechanics
    involved in von Neumann's disproof of the distributive law.

The night before my father left I took him to the cabin at Clear Lake.

As evening came we sat on the pier eating cheese and drinking Red Tails.

Through the silence of conversation I stared into darkness listening for breaths
    that wouldn't come.

My father's risen above the failure of his heart to beat and of his blood to flow.

He's risen above kidney failure and throat cancer and what once seemed to be
    the irrefutable laws of science.

And it was in this way that my father was dead as he raised his hand like a child
    and waved to stars galaxies away and which have been sending
    for countless generations these small drops of light.

V

Hotspot

It's me.
It's where I'm at. Like
right now. It's like you're
half a continent away from me
walking down Boston's Newbury Street with a fashionable
goatee on your chin
considering an early afternoon cocktail at McGreevy's
and even though Marcella who has a diamond-shaped
tattoo on her wrist and speaks with an Italian accent
cuts your hair every five weeks at Viselli's Salon
and even though your Versace Eros cologne
surrounds you with a vanilla-mint aroma
you know as you ask the bartender for a glass
of top-shelf bourbon
that your neatly pressed dress slacks just aren't enough.

Here I am
in northwest Nebraska pouring myself
a late morning bowl of cereal and maybe
there's not enough milk to soak even a quarter
of the corn flakes and maybe the icy wind
won't stop rattling the windows
yet there hovers about me
an invisible cloud of *something*-ness that grooves
like heatwaves—like several hours
of serious shaking at a downtown
night club. It's as if each particle
in the solar system has been funneled to my kitchen
to twirl like a kinetic conga line around my kitchen table
and out my front door.

                    Suddenly you're thinking
Oh, northwest Nebraska! Suddenly
you tell the bartender *Brother,*
I need to get frontier and remote. Who can deny
the electrifying pulse of my town's
solitary stoplight? Who dares assert

EJ's BBQ doesn't have the most secret
secret sauce?

It's like you know
you can't deny
the essential importance of each cow and bull
grazing the unpopulated prairieland
around my house. Though I'm still dressed in my plaid bathrobe
you understand I have traveled lightyears
beyond fashion. You can't deny the flutter of envy
you feel at these miles of unpaved roads
or how intensely you yearn
to experience Anderson Clothing's $8 discount rack.
It's simply impossible for you to ignore
this meteoric surge of rural significance
this dazzling display of High Plains prominence
as I listen to the heater blow and clock tick
and you sip your Four Roses single-barrel bourbon
and order a pork belly taco appetizer
and listen to the buzz of conversation
as the both of us wait
we're always waiting
for whatever it is that's going to happen.

Like Little Steven

Mike backing me down to release his patented baby hook jump shot
in the summer of 2003 is not completely different from Bruce Springsteen

rocking with the E Street Band's Stevie Van Zandt. Like Little Steven,
Bruce's brother-at-arms, that summer I too wore numerous brightly colored
      bandanas.

And even though it wasn't Mike and me sharing vocals on a live performance
of "Ramrod," as our basketball echoed through the neighborhood

the stadium in my mind celebrated our every move.
It was afternoon drives through the Sonoma hills followed by wine bar breaks

at the Oakville Lounge. It was the celebratory chorus of "Darlington County"
blaring from the speakers. And even though Mike was driving

and Bruce singing, sometimes I'd call for a deep cut off *Darkness*
just as Little Steven occasionally stepped into the brightness

of Springsteen's lead-guitar-spotlight. Since he was older
I understood that it had to be Mike who ordered the wine.

The sommelier waited patiently as Mike swirled and sipped a Kenwood
      Cabernet
with expert care. And since he was the better athlete it mattered to both of us

that each of Mike's hook shots resulted in the sweetness of *swoosh*.
These were the days when it was enough for me to experience the pleasures

of bratwurst in Mike's backyard. We relaxed in our denim cutoffs listening
to Bruce's harmonica on the "Promised Land" and as we hiked the Skyline Trail

in early evening and I wore my ornate purple bandana with decorative skulls
it was Mike I followed. It was the certainty in his voice I listened to.

And when Mike suggested we drink one last beer at The Green Lantern
I agreed. And when Mike wanted one more beer after that

I could only say yes. And by late August it could have been Mike
who wrote "Born to Run." Mike—in his own surge of brilliance—capturing the
    chords

Little Steven would help play. Just as it was Bruce
in the coolness of Mike's sunglasses. Bruce turning up the radio

in Mike's Honda Civic. Bruce singing in his gravelly voice, my bandana blowing,
assuring me he had everything under control.

Mystery Ride

Not him whisking me out of bed
tossing me with fatherly excitement
into the backseat
for us to cruise the slow hours of our sleepless nights
the lights of suburbia joyfully
rushing past

but me, 42, guiding his shaking arm
into the passenger's seat
helping him reach the awkward seatbelt
around his waist

and because we desire highway
more than conversation
I pull his old convertible onto the entrance ramp
accelerate to 75
let our bodies press against the leather
white lines thinning into threads
the engine propelling us
past factories and crushed Styrofoam cups
past towns with names familiar
as the songs he would sing

and maybe I become a little concerned, Dad,
as we merge onto I-93
so I point out the steakhouse
you took me to like an annual pilgrimage
maybe I suggest we take the next exit
for a couple cups of coffee

but you only roll the window down
stare past the brightness
of the city that never was your city
past silhouettes of buildings
as twilight fades

and when we cross the state line
and I pull into the same rest stop
you stopped at when I was a boy
you refuse to stretch your arthritic legs
to my frustration
you decline a late-night meal of gas station chicken
insisting on eighteen-wheelers
static on the radio
wind flooding through the window

up the Kancamagus Highway
trees leaning so close
we can't see the stars
my eyes grown tired as the headlights
reveal pavement
like veins twisting through mountains

and when I am overwhelmed
after 300 miles
when in a blurry fatigue I stop
at a North Conway motel
and insist that this is our final destination
when I wait in a lobby
that smells like decades of smoke

it is only natural, Dad, I do not see you
get out of the car
and open the driver's side door
it is only natural—even if I do hear you
start the engine—
that I do not turn and run
to the parking lot
comfortable for a few moments
to let you drift away.

Haunted

Each night I wander the city unable to stop thinking of the quarter ounce of weed I never sold your brother—the night I broke his skull instead. I think of the gold watch that slipped easily from his wrist. Past empty car lots, the abandoned shoe factory, each night the same as that cold April evening. Past the same chain-link fence for twenty-nine years, the green dumpster overflowing with trash. The frozen sleet begins at nine o'clock, my feet wet and aching. You have turned my hair grey, have made my shoulders hunch with age, but never is there sleep, never do you allow me to drink a cup of coffee in the morning. Just this walking with the same tire iron hidden in my jacket. My stomach clenches when I pass the police station. Here is the diner I ate at an hour before your brother's death. Hands in my pockets, eyes on the sidewalk, I can't stop moving. Past the rundown house I grew up in. My parents are dead but when you make me look through the living room window there's the pyramid of beer cans my father left on the floor, the top one filled with cigarettes and spit, the black and white television blares. The city bus waits by the curb but you never allow me to take a seat, never let my hands grow warm. As I wander past the industrial park not a single street light turns on. Here are the rusted railroad tracks I can't stop following, my feet shuffling from wooden tie to wooden tie. Ahead the familiar grove of trees, an unlit bridge. Each night I glimpse the same shadow of a body on the ground. You make my hands shake—as I move closer my chest begins to heave. I can't stop thinking of your brother's brain hemorrhaging blood. You make me watch as his forehead turns purple, as his body begins to spasm. Each night you lean me forward, bend me like a doll, to watch your brother's legs kick out again and again.

Somewhere

The whistle sounds through miles of emptiness
as you pause before each sleeping compartment door,
press your face against the rectangle
of frosted glass searching for his heavy eyelids, greasy hair—
your brother's forehead still purple from the tire iron
that cracked his skull. Along the narrow aisle you listen
for his music, his record player, its one working speaker.
Where is his black t-shirt, his jeans worn at the knees, a bag of dope
tucked in the front pocket? In the dining car your mother
blows cool a spoonful of soup, the newspaper's evening edition
spread before her; your Aunt Kathy, comfortable again
beside her, eyes no longer clouded in a morphine haze,
asks the porter for another glass of sherry.
You slide open each washroom door, search closets
for his scuffed sneakers. In the smoking cabin
your grandfather again lights a thin cigar, wears his white Stetson,
but somewhere must be the neighbor's shed
your brother set on fire, his journal etched
with pages of schizophrenic threats. Your grandfather waves,
your mother, her face no longer worn with age, offers her steaming spoon to you,
balances an open palm underneath, but somewhere
must be your brother's pocket knife, the bed—*his bed*—you inherited
in one of the sleeping compartments. Even here he wants
to press the thin blade against your throat. In the baggage car
you examine the shadow behind your grandfather's bicycle, open each drawer
of your mother's antique rosewood dresser. Where are his muddied boots—
his Marlboro baseball cap hung from a hook? Even here you squeeze around
the food cart, open the next car door and stare
out the window, wheels rumbling through darkness, waiting
for his fingers to tap against the glass.

East Montana

Twenty miles outside of town your Adam can't hear
the refrigerator's loud rattle, there's no hardware store for him
to walk the aisles holding a cracked sprinkler head. He drives north
up highway 201, past the sadness of failed towns. Your Adam understands the
grey indifference of factories, the grey-white smoke drifting from smokestacks.
He enters the safety of a cheap motel room—an ashtray on the nightstand,
a rectangle of fluorescent light from the bathroom. How many other anonymous
bodies have slept under these stained sheets? A man yells, a woman yells louder—
but none of it matters because tomorrow there's a different motel room,
takeout pizza, another man and woman in the room next door. Your Adam drifts
through the High Plains, the rolling flatness. And what if she told him
there would be a child? What if she told him only a week before? None of it
       matters
in east Montana. Just roads and highway
where nothing gets named, houses fall into ruin. Night brings cable television
with complimentary HBO. Night offers a free cup of coffee in the lobby.
He wanders the neon glow of a parking lot, two a.m.,
past a rusted car with Arizona plates, a pickup truck with a tarp covering
used furniture in the bed, the wind blows, a motel door slams
as your Adam listens to eighteen-wheelers rumble.
How could anyone—his Eve, *your* Eve—ever think different?

My Other Bruce

You were a different kind of Bruce. Not Springsteen in a pristine white t-shirt
singing about working-class struggles, the soft intimacy
of his vocals in "Factory" encouraging me to memorize each poetic word
but the Supreme Tough Guy in *Die Hard*—John McClane, off-duty police
        officer—
walking in bare feet across bullet-shattered glass
because no true American would let Hans Gruber and his henchmen
take over a state-of-the-art skyscraper.

                        If it wasn't you I saw
at The Candle Pin bowling alley
it was a world of men aspiring to be you—men with tattoos
on their biceps; men whose girlfriends hollered each time
their guy scored a thundering strike; men like you
willing to toss dead bodies out the 36th-story window

to send Hans an undeniable message. How could Springsteen—
the sincere, reflective artist—impress Melissa Cook
in home economics? But when I tried
spinning a ball of pizza dough on my middle finger
there was a sense of your hip masculinity hovering between us.

                                Like all my friends
I memorized the scene when you, hiding on the 27th-floor, challenged Hans
over walkie-talkie with a completely cool, cowboy inspired,
"Yippie-ki-yay, Mother Fucker." That phrase blossomed into a world
of "Yippie-ki-yays."

                Before asking Melissa to homecoming
I stood in front of the boys' bathroom mirror and attempted
a somewhat cocky, almost manly "Yippie-ki-yay."

The greyness of the town, the men barely older than me
walking to factory jobs, the liquor stores open until one all demanded

your carefree toughness. The beat-up shit-kicker
Bob Young drove in twelfth grade might have backfired
each time he shifted into second gear
but still he revved the engine at traffic lights
with a "Yippie-ki-yay" confidence.

                              And when some drunk piss-ant stumbling
to lane fourteen spills beer on your girl—when he stands there
in his drunk idiocy laughing—well, that's when you had no choice
but to drop a "Mother Fucker"
into your "Yippie-ki-yay."

                    The world was cold, Bruce.
Those February mornings walking to school, the raw wind
making my lungs ache. Yes, I had on headphones. Yes, I listened to Springsteen's
well-crafted *Darkness* album. But in a town of abandoned houses
and factory smoke, in a neighborhood of used car lots and dark barrooms
where no one ever looked up,
it was your words, Bruce,
the promised safety of your wry grin,
that somehow got me through.

Waiting Room

In the dream he wants his mother to be in the chair beside him. He wants both of them to be sipping steaming coffee as they wait for his mother's name to be called.

His mother who must be 79—her lungs still aching with cancer.

He senses she is overdue for an examination. That it's been years since the doctor pointed to the tumors on his mother's CT scan results.

It's as if pressing upon the white waiting room walls is a vague recognition he will never again sit beside his mother on the couch.

That they will never again watch the final innings of a Red Sox game.

There's a microwave on the countertop flashing 12:00 o'clock and grey swinging doors across the hallway.

He senses there is something wrong with the swinging doors.

He hears a high-pitched wind rushing between the doors' thin slit.

He looks at a vase without flowers. He looks at two windows that stare into a night without parking lot lights, without cars driving the streets beyond.

He knows there are no streets beyond.

And it's cold.

So cold it feels as if snow might drift from the fluorescent lights.

So cold, he thinks, that if his mother was beside him she would need to be bundled in a heavy winter jacket. The same winter jacket his mother wore when she drove to the package store for cigarettes at 68.

When she would crack the driver's-side window and let cigarette smoke drift into the winter streets.

Before the doctor assured her surgery was not an option.

Before the doctor suggested they discuss comfort measures.

And now he remembers it's been a decade since he's seen his mother's face. That when walking the hallways at work, when reading a book in the living room, he struggles to recall the sound of his mother's voice.

But even now—ten years later—he wants to see clouds of her breath.

He wants to look upon the redness of his mother's chapped hands as they wait for a nurse to call her name.

A nurse in green scrubs confirming his mother has something to hope for.

Even if the microwave continues to flash.

Even if snow collects at the nurse's feet.

Even if the high-pitched wind rushes through the swinging doors, which he knows—has always known—is really the sound of nothing.

Final Routine

To lessen the overwhelming experience
of her own death my mother
would have gladly turned toward the television which played
in the background during the closing minutes of her life.
If her failing lungs—their irregular,
desperate heaves—allowed her, my mother
would have sat up in the hospital bed
stationed in the middle of the living room
and reached her swollen hand for the discarded remote.
And we her caregivers would have understood
my mother's need to ignore
the obvious shallowness of her breathing
and would have sat silently beside her, our faces reflecting
the blue-green light of the late-night talk show.
As if by attracting our gazes the kind host
with the familiar grin could normalize death
for my mother, those final flutters of her chest,
and make her unwanted experience nothing more
than the simple routine of taking a sip of water,
switching the channel one last time
before sleep's unnoticed arrival.

Driving at Twilight

Let it be late August, Dylan's "Not Dark Yet"
on the radio, those final moments before
I turn the headlights on. Let me hear Dylan's raspy vocals
with only a hint of static. It takes a moment
to realize this is my father's car, the leather seats
of his '62 convertible, a blue air freshener dangling
from the rearview mirror. And maybe I'm a little unsettled
because even now, mind hazy, I know my father's car
is decades gone.

        I coast along the winding streets
of Massachusetts past old colonials soft
with light, streets endlessly empty,
not thinking of my mother's final days—the hospital bed
in the middle of our living room, her erratic inhalations
as my mother's favorite big band music
played on a small radio.

        There's only a rising sense
of the ocean, the scent of sea water. And maybe I realize
my father's actually beside me, that he's been here for miles
wearing a pristine white t-shirt. The static
makes it difficult to hear Dylan
so I turn the radio louder, tap my finger
on the steering wheel. In my father's car
with its long front-end and polished hubcaps
I'm not concerned about the sky's deepening purple,
that the months have faded
from August to November—
the beachfront empty, arcade closed.

        And now it becomes clear
It's really my father who's driving. I now understand
that it's me in the passenger's seat and my mother's
at home. Her body moves like it did at twenty-five, her hair again
dark brown. We do not speak
because my father's got his own favorites playing—Bobby Darin,

Fats Domino. So what if we can barely hear?
So what if the hovering darkness
seems impatient? We're all so young, my father and me,
and my mother too now sitting behind us, her hand reaching
to touch my father's shoulder. We drive
as the ocean moves closer but do not worry
because we have these final threads of purple
and are certain—even as the static grows—
there's something here that will save us.

Acknowledgements

Adelaide Magazine: "His Youth"

Bridge Eight: "Hotspot"

The Cortland Review: "Preferable," "Like Little Steven" (as "Another Bruce Springsteen Poem")

Evening Street Review: "Waiting Room"

Free Lunch: "What Gets Lost"

Hawaii Pacific Review: "Haunted" ("He was the bedroom . . .")

Juked: "In Defense of the McDonald's Corporation as Represented by Ronald McDonald"

Lake Effect: "East Montana"

Lingerpost: "Endless Night"

Little Patuxent Review: "The Next Thirty-Two Years"

Mayday Magazine: "Window Cracked Open"

The Meadow: "My Other Bruce"

New Ohio Review: "The History of Longing"

Nimrod: "The New Physics"

Redactions: "The Idea of North"

Slate: "Seven Ways of Looking at Saint Teresa"

Valparaiso Poetry Review: "Driving at Twilight"

West Trade Review: "Final Routine" and "Haunted" ("Each night I wander the city . . .")

Willow Springs: "My Father's Recitation"

Some of the poems in this collection previously appeared in the chapbook
Driving at Twilight (Main Street Rag).

Thanks to Tamara Toomey, Mike Coughlin, Mark Halliday, Joe Wilkins, Sean
Prentiss, Robert Wrigley, Jill Rosser, Lucas Howell, and Lloyd Schwartz for
their guidance and support.

Steve Coughlin teaches creative writing at Western Colorado University. After receiving his BA from the University of Massachusetts Boston, he received his MFA from the University of Idaho and PhD from Ohio University. Coughlin has published poems and essays in several literary journals and magazines, including the *Gettysburg Review, New Ohio Review, Michigan Quarterly Review, Gulf Coast,* and *Slate.* His other full-length collection of poetry is *Another City* (FutureCycle Press). He lives in Gunnison, Colorado, with his wife and daughter.